THE NEW BF

by Gary Chester

edited by Rick Mattingly

To access audio visit:
www.halleonard.com/mylibrary

Enter Code
7136-4181-1536-4968

20th Printing, April, 2015

ISBN 978-1-4234-1812-2

Published by
Modern Drummer Publications, Inc.
271 Route 46 West
Suite H-212
Fairfield, NJ 07004

Distributed by
Hal Leonard Corporation
7777 W. Bluemound Road
Milwaukee, WI 53213

DEDICATION

This book is dedicated to my wife, Janice, to my daughters Gayle, Jena, Amanda, and Katrina, to my son Timothy, and to all of my other "children": the students who have studied with me over the years, and who helped me prove that my systems work. This book would not have been possible without the help of Chris Adams, who not only painstakingly copied all of the systems and examples, but actually made creative contributions to the project.

Gary Chester

Design and layout:
    David H. Creamer

Assistant editors:
    Susan Hannum
    William F. Miller

Photography:
    Rick Mattingly
    Cover photo taken at Grandslam Studios,
    West Orange, NJ

Special thanks to:
    Ralph Pace, Danny Gottlieb, Steve Ettleson
    and Dick Marcus (Paiste), William F. Ludwig,
    III, Elaine Cannizzaro, Joe Powers, Alan
    Douches, and Glenn Weber

INTRODUCTION

All drummers develop their own patterns, beats and methods of execution as they grow as musicians. However, when playing in the studios they come up against a variety of vastly different musical situations. During my many years in the studio I dealt with many different producers, some of whom played a little bit of drums, and some of whom wanted tricky and unique drum parts. I would take 15 minutes and write the parts out, then play them in the studio, and then take the parts home and file them away. I accumulated quite a few of what I call "systems"—things that weren't based on normal, everyday drum playing. This book illustrates many of these systems, and is designed to develop coordination, musicality, reading ability, and confidence. It also provides drummers with new and exciting material to help them develop individual creativity.

These systems are not designed to be played strictly as exercises, but used as tools to develop new musical ideas. In the studio, you must be prepared to play an incredible variety of musical genres—jazz, rock, Latin, fusion, country, etc. The material contained within these systems can be applied to any and all musical styles

Another aspect of studio playing is sight reading. You should be able to sight-read anything without any problem. Of course, even if you are a great reader, if you come across some tricky patterns and you don't have the coordination to go with the reading, it will throw you. Therefore, the systems in this book will promote advanced reading and coordination not only of single-line drum parts, but multi-line drum parts as well.

The main benefit of mastering these systems, however, is the development of individual creativity. All musicians need inspiration and material to continue their own musical growth. Hopefully, the information contained in these systems will provide you with new possibilities and ideas for continued musical development. The systems will prepare you for things you might encounter in the studio—reading, coordination, flexibility. They will also prepare you to be part of current musical trends, and to create the music of the future.

Current trends in music allow these systems to be used more and more. Once a number of drummers master the systems and can sight-read multi-line drum music, it is possible that composers and arrangers will write music with this approach in mind. It is my hope that, by illustrating these systems, I can help drummers understand their instrument better and help them become members of the "new breed" of drummers who will take part in the shaping of modern music.

CONCEPTS: Part 1

DEVELOPMENT OF ALL LIMBS

One of the biggest problems that many drummers have is the fact that they do not have complete control over all four limbs. Many drummers just practice snare drum exercises and do not incorporate the feet. By the same token, drummers who do incorporate the feet often have trouble leading with the left hand (if they are right-handed). Many drummers come to me and say, "My right hand is fine, but my left hand is terrible." It's the same thing with the feet—strong bass but weak hi-hat. My methods for using these systems cover all aspects of using all four limbs in a practical sense.

RIGHT- AND LEFT-HAND LEAD

All of the systems contained in this book will involve leading with the left hand as well as with the right. This will develop better control over the instrument and eliminate the idea of a weak hand. Most drummers find that, by practicing these exercises with either hand leading, the weaker side becomes the creative side: Since this side is not trained, it is easier for it to groove and play funkier. The concept of left-hand/right-hand lead is especially effective when used with two floor toms and three hi-hats—my concept of "territorial rights." Try to develop a balance in the center of your body, rather than focusing on your right or left.

MY APPROACH TO DRUM SETUP:
"TERRITORIAL RIGHTS"

In my drum setup, I use three hi-hats—two in the traditional position and one on the side above the floor tom. I also use a second floor tom to the left of the traditional hi-hat. I find that this offers tremendous flexibility, and I recommend using a similar setup when practicing these systems.

By using three hi-hats, you are opening up a whole new world of possibilities. You can lead with the right hand on the closed right hi-hat, and play patterns, beats, and accents on the drums, cymbals, or other hi-hat to create a variety of feels and tonal colors. You can also lead with the left and have right-hand flexibility. I call this approach "open arms": right-hand lead on the right hi-hat; left-hand lead on the left hi-hat. Crossing over the snare drum to play the hi-hat seems unnatural to me.

This brings us to the second floor tom, and the idea of territorial rights. I use the second floor tom (on the left side) for many sound possibilities. I find it easy to simulate two bass drums by tuning the tom to the same pitch as the bass drum. It is also very useful when leading with the left hand.

"Territorial rights" refers to playing the instruments on the left side with the left hand, and playing the instruments on the right side with the right hand.

As you can see from the photo, the small tom, hi-hat, cymbals, snare, and large tom (on the left) are most naturally played by the left hand, while the snare, small tom, large tom, hi-hat and cymbals on the right are played by the right hand. It is simple and logical. If you put a four-year-old child behind a set of drums, the child would not cross over to play the hi-hat.

I found that one of the biggest problems I had in the studio (as far as technical execution) was ending a fill on the right side and then getting back to the hi-hat. By using three hi-hats, two floor toms, and left- and right-hand leads, this is no longer a problem. Be sure that you use the same setup when you play that you use when you practice.

BASS DRUM TECHNIQUE

Many drummers wonder whether they should play the bass drum with the heel down or up. I feel that for today's music you need to be able to play both ways.

I personally play with the heel down, and my power comes from the knee down, not from the hip. During my years in the studio, we very rarely played very loudly, and engineers were able to adjust my sound to whatever volume was needed.

However, today's studio playing, as a rule, is much louder. With the invention of modern recording instruments, such as limiters, and the success of heavy rock bands, you are often called upon to play very loudly. Studio engineers today call the bass drum a kick drum, and many times that is what you do—kick it! I find that playing with the heel up gives you a short, staccato sound, and playing with the heel down gives you a more rounded sound. You will need to be able to play at all dynamic levels, so you should practice both methods. I, however, recommend more concentrated effort on the heel-down approach for control.

POSTURE

I'm a firm believer in sitting properly when you practice, play in the studio, or perform live. Good posture will help you keep your stamina and endurance, and prevent possible back injury.

In the studio, I would sometimes work 17- to 20-hour days. In 1969, I suffered a slipped disc injury and was out of work for six months. Although I felt that my posture was okay, being more aware of specifics in this area might have helped to prevent this injury.

Another benefit of sitting correctly relates to hearing the instrument. Sitting with correct posture allows you to hear the entire set, as opposed to when you are leaning over the hi-hat or snare drum. It also enables you to play with a very natural balance of sound between each part.

I suggest using a mirror when you practice. You can check your posture, and even your facial expressions. Some students bite their lips or stick their tongues out. That just dissipates your energy.

TIME

The most important thing for a drummer is understanding time. This occurs with experience and dedicated practice. There are three basic time feels: on top, in the middle, and behind. You have to find out which time feel works in a particular situation.

On Top—This type of feel generates the most energy and excitement, but there is always a danger of rushing. In playing on top of the beat, you play with a feel slightly in front of the center of the beat.

In The Middle—This type of time feel is exactly that: in the middle of the beat.

Behind—This feel places the groove slightly behind the center of the beat. Playing with Count Basie requires playing behind.

In playing good time with a rhythm section, the bass player and drummer must work well together. It is great if you can find a bass player who you are comfortable with—one who feels time in the same place that you do. Then the two of you can figure out the type of feel required for a given session.

In practicing the systems, you should practice with a click track, because in the studio you must be able to work with it. People say that a metronome doesn't swing. It doesn't, but what you put with it will swing. Practicing the systems with a click will help develop a good sense of time, and will help develop the feel of working with a click. Practice the systems using all three types of time feels.

GROOVE AND SWING

The way to make these systems cook is to know them inside out. When reading a chart for the first time, just about any drummer, even one of the greats, will sound mechanical. But by the third or fourth time through, it should groove. The same idea applies to these systems. The first time you play it, it's not going to swing. These are coordinating exercises, and they are hard. They will be (for the most part) unfamiliar to you, and nothing unfamiliar is going to cook right away. After you understand each system, sing each line, and hear and understand all the lines and parts. Then you can work on specifics about the groove.

After you can play each system reasonably well, tape yourself. Listen for spacing, sound, accents, dynamics, and musical approach. Criticize yourself to the x degree.

Grooving in the studio or with a rhythm section is not a one-person thing. You can practice grooving at home and play great. However, you might get with a rhythm section in which the bass player plays something that contradicts what you are playing, and the groove will be gone. There are many aspects to playing a groove. Bass, guitar, drums and keyboards all must groove together. Therefore, it is important to practice so that what you play feels good to you, but it is also important to get experience with other musicians and work on grooves together.

THE IMPORTANCE OF SINGING

This concept represents one of the most important and beneficial ways of using the systems. As you go through the systems, you will find that you have to sing various parts of the exercises. You will end up using the voice almost like a fifth limb, and this will help you in many ways. Some of them are:

1. *Ability to hear and feel the quarter note.* One of the first things you have to sing is the quarter note, along with the metronome, as you sight-read. The quarter note is the daddy of the bar; singing it really helps you hear exactly where the quarter is, and how everything you play relates to it. This will result in better time feel and better execution.

2. *Sight-reading ability.* As you advance through the systems, you will find yourself playing with all four limbs and singing a different part each time you play through an exercise. As you sight-read, you will sing the quarter note, then the snare drum part, then the line you are sight-reading, and in some cases, the upbeat and the hi-hat or cymbal part. Practicing in this manner helps you to sight-read without having to sing the melody line all the time, and enables you to recognize figures and execute them instinctively.

3. *Understanding of individual parts.* When playing complicated figures with all four limbs, you must be aware of each individual part that makes up the figure. In the studio, you may sometimes be asked to play the bass drum louder or the snare drum softer. You may find that, by changing just one part of the figure that you are playing, such as simplifying the snare drum or playing a part on the hi-hat instead of the snare, you can create a special effect or please a producer. By practicing these systems while singing a specific part, you will become acutely aware of each part, and thus be able to have more control over dynamics and more flexibility when you are playing.

4. *Alleviate mechanical reading.* Many drummers sight-read well, but they are not really hearing and feeling what they are playing because they are playing mechanically. By mastering the systems and being able to sing each part, sight reading will become less mechanical and more musical. You will be so familiar with figures that coordination and execution will not be a problem; you will be free to create a feel within the music you are sight-reading.

5. *Awareness of pitch and timbre.* When singing each individual part, you should sing in a tone very close to the part that you are focusing on. The snare drum vocal part should sound somewhat like a snare, bass drum like a bass drum, etc. Many drummers are not aware of tones and pitches. Most can hear a snare drum part, but when asked to play the same figure between tom-toms or on the bass drum, they are lost. When practicing the systems, you will find melodic lines shifting around among different instruments. Singing these different parts enables you to understand fully each tone color.

6. *Awareness of spacing.* Singing helps you to be aware of the placement of each beat and the spaces between each note. A common problem is rushing fills when excited. Singing will help you develop an accurate awareness of spacing and precise execution. Some of my students, after mastering the singing of each part, sing the rests while playing the exercise.

7. *Energy.* Singing can create a certain excitement and energy when you are practicing, playing in an isolation booth in the studio, or playing in a live performance situation. When you sing with energy, you play with energy.

8. *Breathing.* Another benefit that results from singing exercises is awareness of correct breathing. Try to sing a drum fill while breathing in. It is incredibly awkward. The fill flows naturally when you release the air. I feel that, if you breathe normally, your playing will flow normally.

A concept that helps many students is the idea of breathing in the same manner that a horn player breathes. Sometimes I have students write breath marks in each exercise to promote natural breathing.

The concept of singing will become more understandable as you go through the systems. Hopefully, you will find that this is a very enjoyable and beneficial part of your practice routine.

39 SYSTEMS

The following pages contain 39 basic patterns, called "systems," followed by ten pages of reading material, which are to be used as the "melodies" for each system.

Start by memorizing the system, being careful to play the correct instrument with the correct hand or foot. You will not be playing the melody yet, but be sure to notice where you are eventually to play it. Play the system many times, striving to make it feel as good as possible. While you are playing the system, sing the click pulse (quarter notes).

After you have memorized a system, turn to the first two Reading pages (14 and 15) and play them as the Melody of the system, on the instrument that is specified with each system. After you can play both pages from beginning to end comfortably, proceed to the second set of Melodies, and practice them the same way.

It is not intended that you rush through any of this material. Do not proceed onward until you have achieved total mental and physical independence and awareness with each system.

To aid your awareness, you should learn to sing each part that you are playing, in addition to singing the click pulse. In other words, while playing the complete System with Melody, sing (1) the click pulse, (2) the melody, (3) the snare drum line, (4) the cymbal line, (5) the hi-hat line, etc.

When singing, it helps to sing a sound that resembles the particular instrument, and to sing it as rhythmically as possible *out loud*. For example, the bass drum part might sound like "boom," while you might sing the hi-hat part with a "chick" sound.

The following abbreviations are used in this book:

H.H. = hi-hat   Ride = ride cymbal (or additional closed hi-hat)
Bell = cymbal bell   B.D. = bass drum   Fl. tom = floor tom

Melody = Reading exercise pages

L.H. = Left hand   R.H. = Right hand
L. F. = Left foot   R.F. = Right foot

Examples:
R.H./Ride = Right hand on ride cymbal (or closed hi-hat)
L.H./Fl. tom = Left hand on floor tom
R.F./B.D./Melody = Right foot on bass drum plays melody
L.F./H.H. = Left foot on hi-hat

PRACTICE TIPS FOR SYSTEMS

I suggest practicing each bar at least four times, or as many times as it takes to get a good understanding of what you are playing. Start slowly and relax. The tendency is to rush through each measure and get right to the end. That is not the point of the exercise, although you will be able to do that after you have mastered each individual measure.

After you become familiar with the technical-coordination aspect of each system, then you can work on feel, groove, dynamics, and application for a variety of musical situations. For example, you could pretend that the line you are sight-reading on the bass drum is a horn melody line, and play everything with the hands dynamically as though you were setting up a big band.

When you read these systems in practice, try to read the phrases across as you would sight-read a page of music—not up and down. By this I mean that most people relate each note to where it falls in relation to the quarter note. It is good to feel this when you sing, but I do not recommend trying to read against the quarter.

These systems all work together. Try to work through them in order, as they are designed to be practiced that way. Master these systems and you will have an incredible variety of musical ideas, to be called upon as you need them.

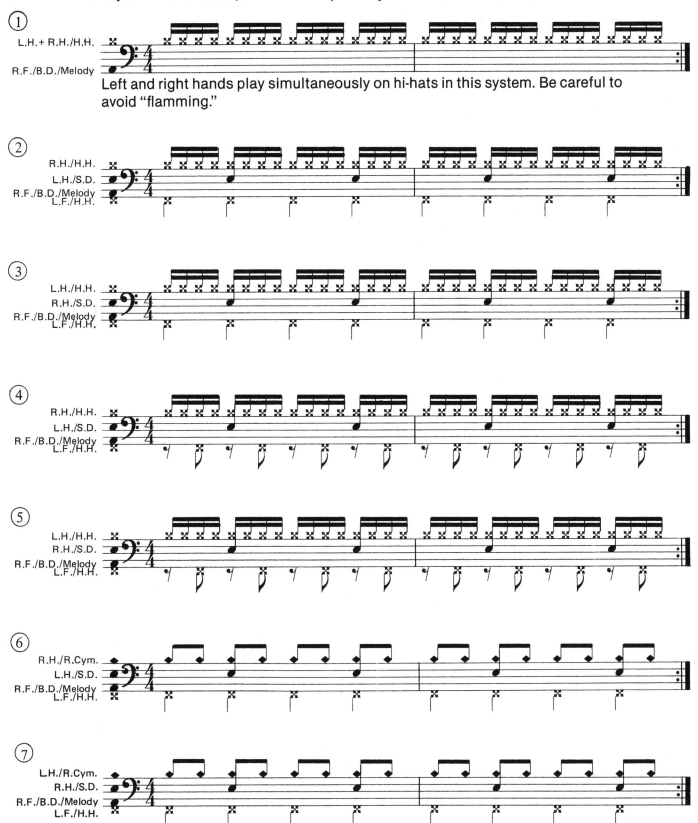

Left and right hands play simultaneously on hi-hats in this system. Be careful to avoid "flamming."

11

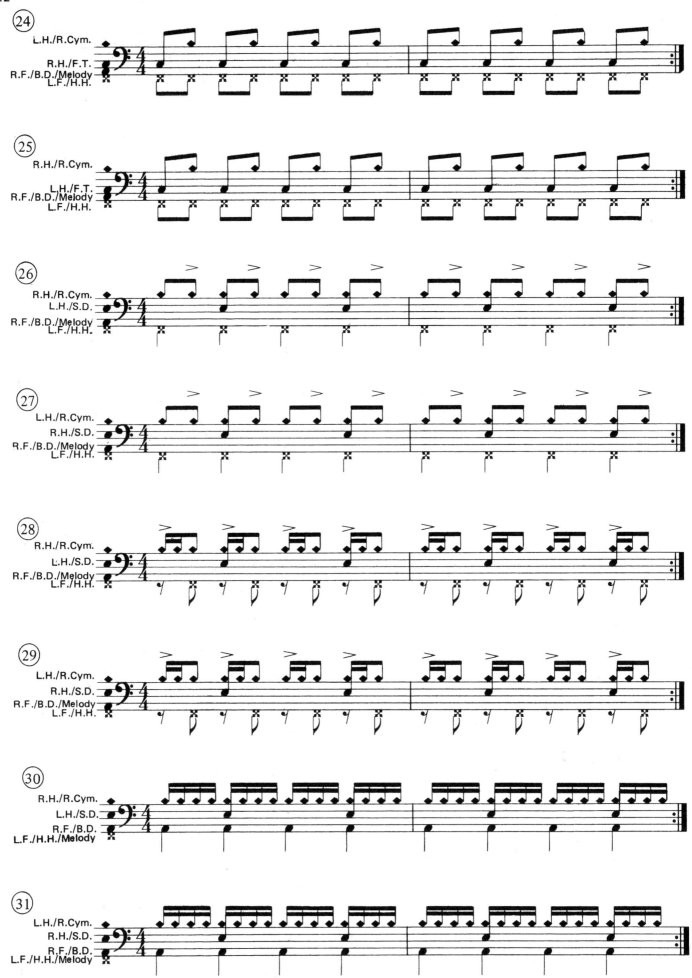

READING

The following pages are to be used as the "melodies" for the systems.

I-A

I-B

II-A

II-B

III-A

III-B

IV-A

IV-B

V-A

V-B

ADVANCED SYSTEMS

The following pages contain ten advanced systems, followed by ten additional pages of reading. Be sure to follow the instructions for each system carefully. Some of them involve playing the melody on snare drum, while others call upon you to play an alternating pattern with your hands between the snare drum and hi-hat.

The singing instructions for the first 39 systems apply to this section of the book as well. Singing is an important part of this entire learning process, and it shouldn't be overlooked.

The reading examples in this section are based on two-bar phrases, each of which is repeated. At first, you might want to concentrate on one two-bar phrase at a time. But eventually, you should be able to play straight through the entire page without stopping.

These reading pages can also be used with the first 39 systems. Similarly, reading pages I-A through V-B can be used with the ten advanced systems. Remember that the ultimate goal is to be able to sight-read a melody line while playing a system, so do not stop with the reading exercises in this book. Take other reading books, such as Ralph Pace's *Variations Of Drumming*, Ted Reed's *Syncopation*, Danny Pucillo's *New Concepts Of Reading Drum Music*, or Louie Bellson and Gil Breines' *Modern Reading Text In 4/4*, and practice reading the rhythms in those books while playing the systems in this book.

5a

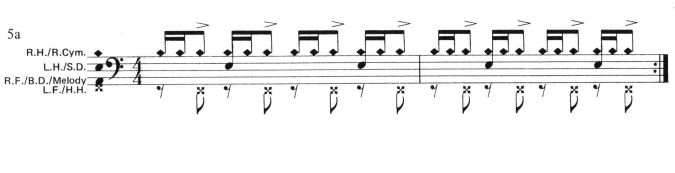

6a

7a

8a

9a

10a

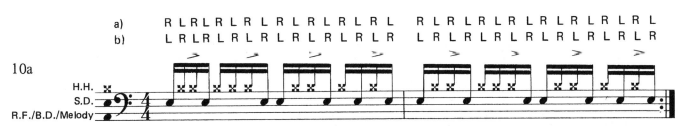

If you have a third hi-hat, you can play upbeats with your left foot on systems 9a and 10a.

ADVANCED READING
EXERCISE 1

EXERCISE 2

EXERCISE 3

EXERCISE 4

EXERCISE 5

EXERCISE 6

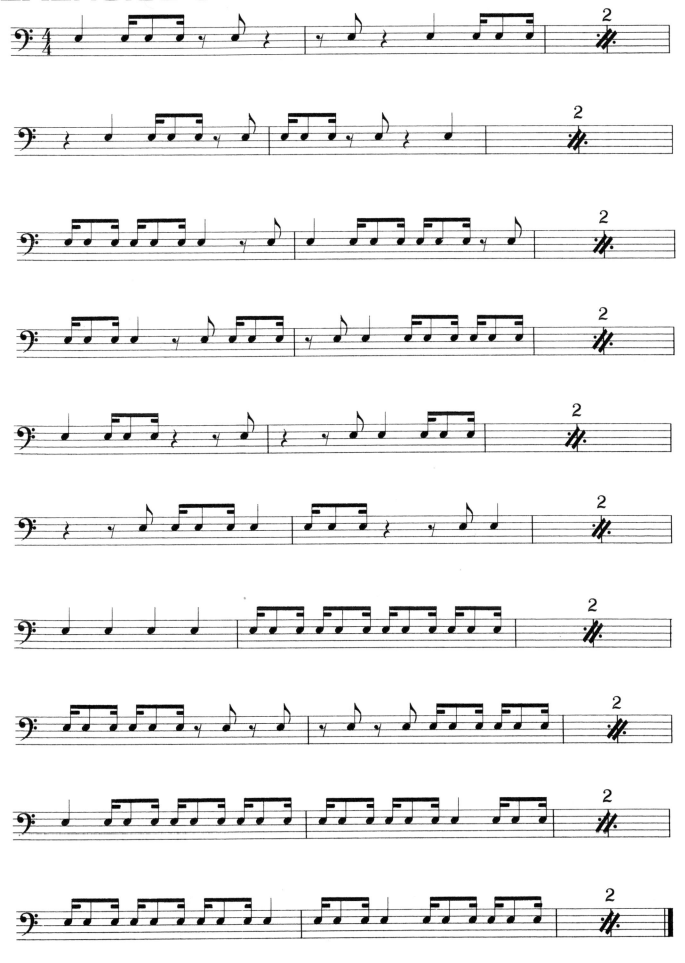

EXERCISE 7

EXERCISE 8

EXERCISE 9

EXERCISE 10

CONCEPTS: Part 2

CONCENTRATION

You will find that mastering the systems requires a lot of concentration. You are singing one part and sight-reading another. It is hard, but you will find it easier as you go through the systems. You will find that it is also very helpful in developing concentration for precision in the studio or in performance.

One student in describing a lesson with me once said, "When I go for a lesson with you, Gary, the dogs come in and out, your wife comes in, the phone rings, three students are in there hanging around for their lessons—all in the same room while I'm having my lesson. Do you expect me to concentrate through all of that?" My answer was, "Absolutely." You should have confidence in yourself and be able to concentrate on what you are doing, no matter who is watching, or listening, or what's going on around you. It's hard, but it's worth working towards this goal.

CONFIDENCE

After you master these systems, you will feel a certain satisfaction in knowing that you can play some very complicated and exciting things. A problem, however, is remembering that many times you will be required to play simply. This becomes a problem because you have so much that you are able to play, but something simple is what works. Sometimes what you play is what makes something musical; sometimes it's what you don't play. The confidence comes in knowing that you can cover any musical situation, from something simple to something complex.

TUNING OF DRUMS

Studio equipment and techniques are constantly changing and improving. They have come a long way from the old two-, three-, and four-track recordings of the 1960s. When I was actively involved in studio playing, each studio had a different sound; each isolation booth was different. I would bring my own drums, and tune specifically for each studio.

You still need to tune your drums for each studio situation, but with today's advanced studio technology, a major factor is the engineer. My advice is to get as much playing experience in the studio as possible, and learn as much about modern recording techniques as you can. Become familiar with microphones, placement, and equalization. Also, listen to the drum sound in the booth during playbacks. Ask questions and discuss the drum sound with the engineer. In this manner, you will familiarize yourself with the type of drum sound that you need. In playing these systems, tune the drums so they sound great to you, and are enjoyable to play. You must feel comfortable with the sound of the instrument.

I've been recommending that my students get small, portable P.A. systems and microphones for their drums for small-club use and practice. In large concerts, of course, this is not needed, as the P.A. systems usually cover drum amplification and monitoring. However, today's modern playing demands well-defined drum sounds, and a small portable P.A. fits the need perfectly. That way you do not have to strain to increase your volume. You can hear every note you play no matter how loud the rest of the band is, and you can enjoy a full, rounded drum sound. Also, you can add effects such as delay and reverb for interesting sounds. Therefore, you can keep the balance, energy, etc., that you worked so hard to get. Remember, it doesn't have to be loud to have energy.

READING

In the studio, you find a large variety in the types of drum parts. You can get a lead sheet, which consists of chords and melody, and that is the same part for all members of the rhythm section. You may get a drum part with minimal figures and cues on it, or you may get a complicated, fully written out drum part. It is important to become aware of what these parts represent, and then develop skills at interpreting these charts to play musically and creatively.

Arrangers who know you and know how well you read might write out exactly what they want you to play. By the same token, they might not write anything for you, because they know that you will come up with a groove or feeling that is better than anything they can write. This approach allows the innovative talent of the drummer to surface. Writing a simple drum part by knowing a particular drummer's skills makes an arranger's job a lot easier.

There is another type of arranger who writes a very complicated drum part for you, figuring that if it doesn't work, parts can be eliminated. However, I've found from experience that, with a complicated part, it normally takes a lot longer to get a good groove. Usually, what you must do in a situation like this is use your ears, and your musical and technical ability to figure out what works for what the arranger really wants. Most of the time, you can find something that you are comfortable with and that also works for the arranger. Mastering these systems will increase your vocabulary of possibilities.

Very few recording arrangers really know what a drummer can do, so they usually write parts that tend to be simplistic to protect themselves and the session. Experience, sensitivity, confidence and proper attitude are the most important aspects of dealing with studio situations.

LISTENING

Successful studio musicians don't lock into one type of music. They are aware of all types—jazz, fusion, rock, country, pop, R&B—and can play them all authentically. Learning about these styles comes from listening extensively to all types of music, and knowing what is called for.

A problem in playing along with records is the fact that, since the drum part and time feel are already established, you are following along. But that can also be beneficial from an analytical point of view. You can learn what the great drummers do in a particular musical situation, learn from it, and apply it to your own playing.

DEVELOPING CREATIVITY

You must figure out for yourself how far you want to go. There are no rules, just endless possibilities for musical development. One person will practice just a little; others will practice eight hours a day. Some will be professional musicians and musical innovators; others will play for fun on weekends. It's all up to you to take it to whatever level you desire.

All of your deficiencies will surface during practice sessions, but that is what practicing is for. Some people get bored when they practice. I feel that boredom comes from not being able to concentrate, for whatever reason. Some people just don't like hard things, others are lazy, while for others, being a professional musician is not the right thing. It's all up to you.

No two drummers approach music the same way. No two drummers will play and apply these systems in the same way. What I do hope, though, is that these systems will provide you with some fresh ideas to develop your own creativity, so that you can take part in forging new directions in music, making you an important part of the "New Breed."

COMPOSITE SYSTEMS

The possibilities for creating new systems is endless. One way is to select a cymbal, snare drum and hi-hat pattern from one of the given systems, and then to select a bass drum pattern from one of the reading exercises. For example, take the cymbal, snare and hi-hat part from system 28, and play the first measure of reading III-A on the bass drum.

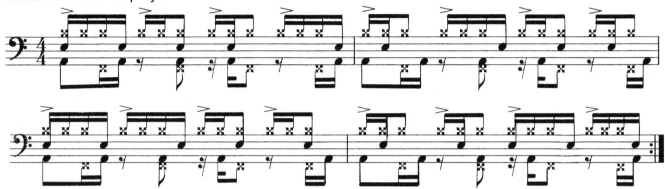

After you can play this system comfortably, practice reading the melodies on the snare drum. Using the system given above, and reading III-A with it, the first four measures would be played as follows:

You should practice all of the reading pages with that same cymbal, snare drum and hi-hat pattern.

Once you are comfortable with that, use the second measure of III-A as the bass drum pattern, and repeat the process. Here's how that system would look with the first four bars of reading II-B.

As you go through the various reading pages in this manner, you will discover patterns that you particularly like, as well as some that you don't. Go back to the ones you like and use them. Also, don't be afraid to inject your own ideas—an extra note or two, open hi-hat effects, or whatever. That's how you develop your own creativity, and your own musical personality.

The following pages contain several combinations of systems and reading exercises, to give you an idea of what is possible. Certainly you should spend time working on the examples that are given, but don't stop there. I am only giving you four measures at a time. Be sure to go back to the actual reading pages and develop the ability to read the entire page while playing the system. Also, be sure to continue to develop your own systems, based on the procedure shown in this chapter. If you only play the patterns given in the book, you'll just be a Gary Chester clone, and frankly, the world doesn't need any of those. Be your own person by developing your own ideas.

COMPOSITE SYSTEM 1

System 2

Reading I-A, measure 8

Composite system 1

Composite system 1 with first four measures of reading I-A on snare drum.

COMPOSITE SYSTEM 2

System 4

Reading I-B, measure 21

Composite system 2

Composite system 2 with first four measures of reading I-B on snare drum.

COMPOSITE SYSTEM 3

System 6

R.H./R.Cym.
L.H./S.D.
L.F./H.H.

Reading II-A, measure 12

Composite system 3

Composite system 3 with first four measures of reading II-A on snare drum.

COMPOSITE SYSTEM 4

System 8

R.H./R.Cym.
L.H./S.D.
L.F./H.H.

Reading II-B, measure 9

Composite system 4

Composite system 4 with first four measures of reading II-B on snare drum.

COMPOSITE SYSTEM 5

System 10   Reading III-A, measure 27

Composite system 5

Composite system 5 with first four measures of reading III-A on snare drum.

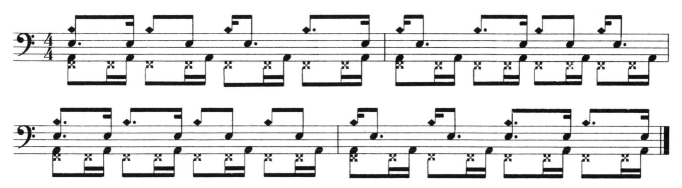

COMPOSITE SYSTEM 6

System 12   Reading III-B, measure 29

Composite system 6

Composite system 6 with first four measures of reading III-B on snare drum.

COMPOSITE SYSTEM 7

System 14

Reading IV-A, measure 10

Composite system 7

Composite system 7 with first four measures of reading IV-A on floor tom.

COMPOSITE SYSTEM 8

System 11

Reading IV-B, measure 5

Composite system 8

Composite system 8 with first four measures of reading IV-B on snare drum.

COMPOSITE SYSTEM 9

System 7

L.H./R.Cym.
R.H./S.D.
L.F./H.H.

Reading V-A, measure 3

Composite system 9

Composite system 9 with first four measures of reading V-A on snare drum.

COMPOSITE SYSTEM 10

System 5

L.H./H.H.
R.H./S.D.
L.F./H.H.

Reading V-B, measure 29

Composite system 10

Composite system 10 with first four measures of reading V-B on snare drum.

GARY'S GROOVES

Obviously, a lot of the systems and patterns used in this book are more for practice and development than they are for grooves that can be played in real situations. But by practicing those exercises, you will gain the technique and control of the instrument necessary for you to create your own grooves. The following are some grooves that I particularly like. They are based on techniques that are developed by the systems, but they also include things like accents and open/closed hi-hat effects. You may like some of these grooves; you may not like others. That's not important. What is important is that you go on to create your own grooves and patterns.

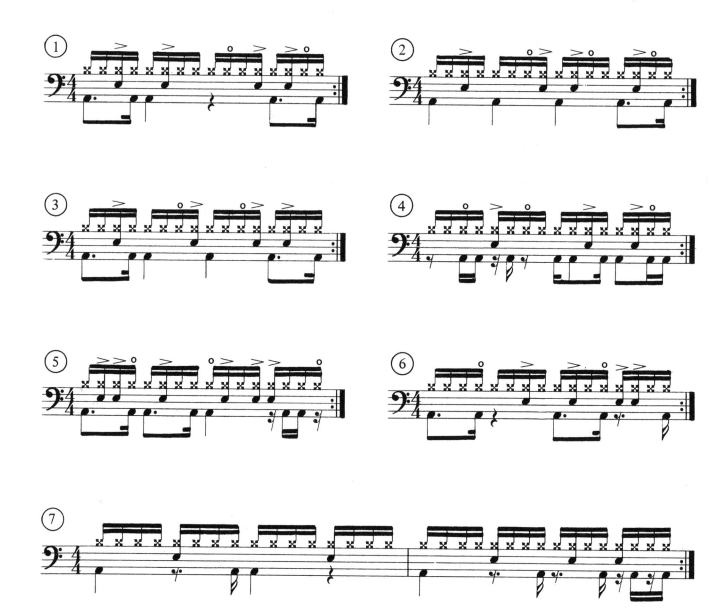

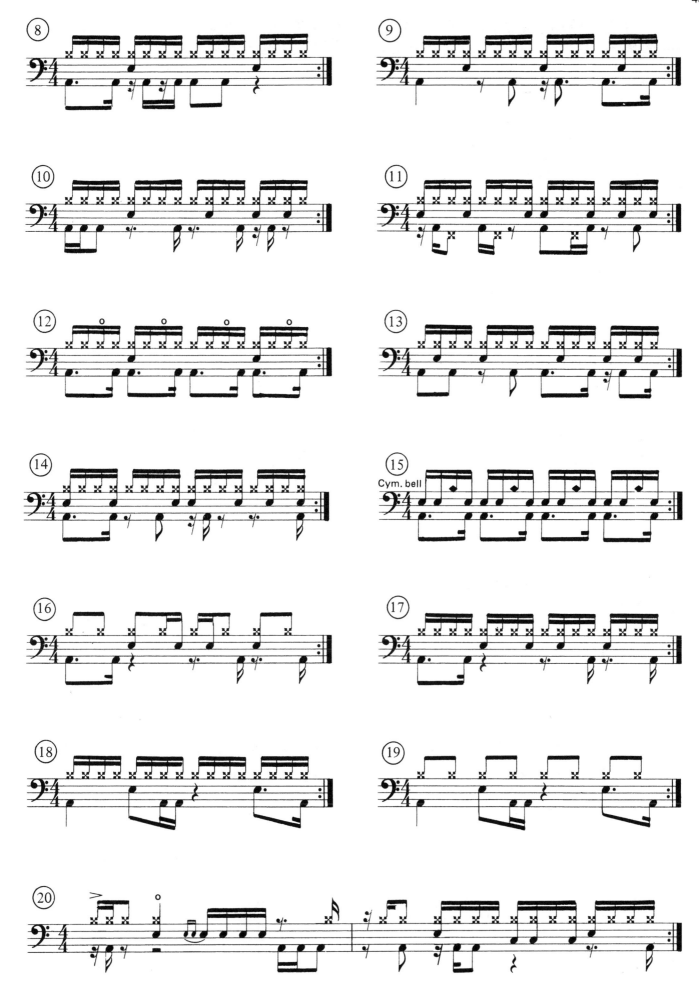

APPLICATIONS

The following groove was played by drummer Dave Weckl in the tune "Gdansk," on the Paquito DiRivera album, *Why Not?* It demonstrates a practical application of the systems, especially the use of "territorial rights."

The following excerpt, again by Dave Weckl, is from the Bill Conners album *Step It.* This section occurs during the guitar solo on the tune "Cookies," and shows a practical application of multiple hi-hats.

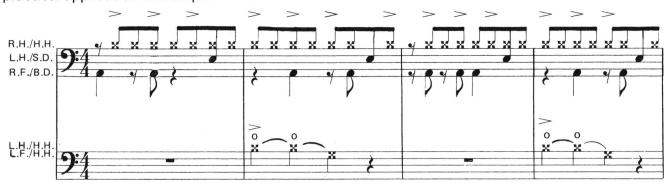

Drummer Howard Joines used double hi-hats when he played the Broadway show *Little Shop Of Horrors*, as shown here.

"LITTLE SHOP"

"DA-DOO"

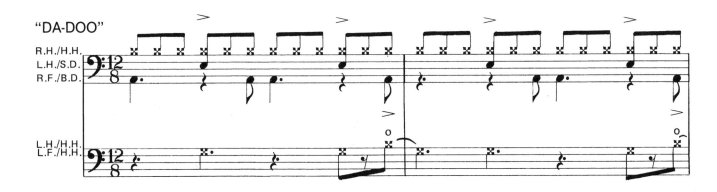

CREDITS

Gary Chester played on the following hit records and albums:

Angels—"My Boyfriend's Back"
Paul Anka—"Let's Sit This One Out" / "My Broken Heart" / "I'm Coming Home" / "Miranda" / "I'll Never Find Another You" / "All Of Me" / "Cry" / "Esso Besso" / "It Only Lasts For A Little While" / "Hush Hush My Broken Heart" / "I'm Coming Home" / "I Need You Now" / "Send For Me" / "Pretend"
The Archies—*Sugar, Sugar*
Burt Bacharach—"Promises, Promises" / "Reach Out" / "Alfie" / "Make It Easy On Yourself"
LaVerne Baker—"Saved" / "You're The Boss"
Tony Barra—*Red, White And Blue*
Vinnie Bell Orchestra—*Big Sixteen / Pop Goes The Electric Guitar*
Belmonts—"When Your Lover Has Gone" / "Farewell" / "Walk Down The Road" / "I'll Be Seeing You"
Willie Bobo—*Let's Go Bobo*
Lillian Briggs—"I Want You"
Ruth Brown—"Naturally" / "Anyone But You" / "Sure Enough" / "Here He Comes"
Anita Bryant—"Love Letters In The Sand" / "Misty" / *All The Way*
Solomon Burke—"Walking In The Footsteps" / "A Tear Fell" / "Cry To Me" / "Almost Lost My Mind" / "I Really Don't Want To" / "My Heart Is Crying" / "Home" / "You Can Make It If You Try"
Artie Butler—*Have You Met Mrs. Jones* / "Freedom"
Al Caiola—*The Best Of Al Caiola / Tuff Guitars / Lovers Guitars*
Cab Calloway—*Cab Calloway '68*
The Chiffons—"He's So Fine"
Jimmy Clanton—"Just A Dream"
Petula Clark—"Downtown"
Buzz Clifford—"Magic Circle" / "Moving Day" / "Castaways"
The Coasters—"Little Egypt" / "Wait A Minute" / "Thumbing A Ride"
Amanda Cole—"Miss Happiness" / "The Image Of Me" / "Heartbreak USA" / "If You Could Read My Mind"
Cozy Cole (w/Gary Chester)—"Swinging Drummer"
Cy Coleman—*The Age Of Rock*
Perry Como—*No Other Love*
The Cookies—"Chains" / "Stranger In My Arms"
Don Costa—*Hully Gully Time* / "Honeysuckle Rose" / "Sugar Blues"
Country Joe & The Fish—*Dr. Hip / Rhymes & Reasons*
The Crests—"16 Candles"
Jim Croce—"Time In A Bottle" / *Bad, Bad, Leroy Brown* / "I Love You With A Song" / "Operator" / *Croce / Photographs And Memories*
The Crystals—"Gee Whiz" / "Look In My Eyes" / "Frankenstein Twist" / *Uptown* / "Seventeen"
Johnny Cymbal—"Mr. Bass Man"
Bobby Darin—*Artificial Flower* / "My Foolish Heart" / "Street Where You Live" / "Theme From Come September" / "Moon River" / "Someone Special" / "Dream Lover" / "At Last" / "All In The Game" / "Will You Love Me Tomorrow" / "Ya Ya"
Delta Rhythm Boys—"Little Jimmy From Texas" / "Bewitched"
John Denver—"Rocky Mountain High" / *Prayers & Promises / Farewell Andromeda / Airie*
Jackie DeShannon—"What The World Needs Now"
The Devotions—"How Do You Speak To An Angel"
The Dials—"The Start Of A New Romance"
The Drifters—"Up On The Roof" / "Under The Boardwalk" / "I Count The Tears" / "Some Kind Of Wonderful" / "Please Stay" / "Roomful Of Tears" / "I'll Take You Where The Music Is Playing" / "Save The Last Dance For Me" / "When My Little Girl Is Smiling"
Bobby Dukeoff—*On The Cuff*
The Edsels—"You Know I Do" / "Pillow Could Talk" / "Shake Shake Sherry"
Les Elgart—*The Twist Goes To College*
The Everly Brothers—"Crying In The Rain"
Exciters—"Tell Him"
Ferrante & Teicher—*Killing Me Softly / Midnight Cowboy / Piano Portraits*
The Five Satins—"Still Of The Night"
The Four Coins—"To Love" / "Moon Of Monacuri" / "Wide Wide World" / "Wish You Were Here" / "Windows Of Heaven" / "I Believe" / "You Will Never Walk Alone" / "Little Bit Closer" / "From Your Very Own Lips"
Connie Francis—"I'm Gonna Be Warm This Winter" / "Movie Queen" / "Playing Games" / "Saturday Night" / "Give Me Back My Heart" / "Ain't That Better Baby" / "Don't Cry On My Shoulder" / "Love Bird" / "Pray For Me" / "Lonely Star" / "Please Do Go" / "The Girl In Me" / "Castle In The Sky" / "Half Heaven, Half Heartache" / "Silver And Gold" / "I Don't Need You" / "Puddle Of Love" / "Your Skies Of Blue"
Aretha Franklin—*Rockaby My Baby* / "God Bless The Child" / "Kiss Under The Mistletoe" / "Ask About You" / "How Deep Is The Ocean" / "Silver Lining" / "I'm Sitting On Top Of The World" / "Lover Come Back"
Irma Franklin—*Her Name Is Irma / Hello Again*
Astrid Gilberto—*I Haven't Got Anything Better To Do*
Bobby Goldsboro—*Raindrops Are Falling* / "In The Autumn Of Your Life"
Leslie Gore—"It's My Party"
Living Guitars—*Teen Beat*
Joel Harnel—*Fly Me To The Moon*
Bob Hayley—"Doesn't Anybody Make Short Movies Anymore" / "Tonight You Belong To Me" / "The Key To Room 303" / "You're Nobody Till Somebody Loves You"
Richard Hayman—*Cinemagic Sounds*
Hedge & Donna—*All The Friendly Colors / Hedge & Donna II*
Daphne Hellman—*Holiday For Hay*
George Hudson—*It's Twisting Time*
Brian Hyland—*Sealed With A Kiss* / "Pledging My Love" / "Devoted To You" / "Let Me Belong To You" / "Let It Die"
Isley Brothers—"Twist And Shout" / "Your Old Lady Is My Old Lady Too" / "Write To Me" / "I'm A Fool For You" / "One More Time"
Cook E. Jarr—*Pledging My Love* / "Sweet Little You"
Jay & The Americans—*Stand By Me / She Cried* / "Spanish Harlem" / "Come A Little Bit Closer" / "Cara Mia"
Jack Jones—"Party" / "Dreaming All The Time" / "Gift Of Love" / "Pick Up The Pieces"
Quincy Jones—*Hash Brown*
Sammy Kaye—"Charades"
Jim Kersich & The Jug Band—*Garden Of Joy*
Ben E. King—"Spanish Harlem" / "Don't Play That Song" / "Stand By Me" / "Here Comes The Night" / "Yes" / "Ecstasy" / "Amor"
Ben Lanzaroni—*In Classic Form*
Curtis Lee—"Angel Eyes" / "Beverly Gene" / "Lonely Weekend" / "Just Another Fool" / "A Night At Daddy G's"
Little Anthony & The Imperials—"Out Of My Head" / "Tears On My Pillow"
Little Eva—"Locomotion"
Gloria Loring—*And Now We Come To Distances*
Lovin' Spoonful—"Do You Believe In Magic"
George Maharis—"Fools Rush In" / "Love Me As I Love You" / "Love Me Tender" / "Warm All Over"
Barry Mann—*Bless You* / "The Way Of A Clown" / "Foot Steps"
Manhattan Transfer—*Fair And Tender Ladies*
Ray Martin—*Comic Strip Favorites*
Chuck Marshall—*Twist To Songs Everybody Knows*
Clyde McPhatter—"It's A Lover's Question" / "Crying Won't Help You Now"
The Mellow Kings—"Walk Softly" / "But You Lied" / "Things I Love" / "Broken Heart Symphony"
Garnett Mims—*Cry Baby*
The Monkees—"I'm A Believer"
Lou Monte—"What Did Washington Say"
Jane Morgan—*What Now My Love / Jane Morgan In Gold*
Van Morrison—"Brown Eyed Girl" / *T. B. Sheets*
Buddy Morrow—*Beatlemania*
Murray The K—"Lonely Twister" / "Twisting Up A Storm"
Jimmy Mundy—*On A Mundy Flight*
Anthony Newley—"What Kind Of Fool Am I" / "Claire De Lune" / "A Lock Of Hair" / "Talk Of The Town"
Wayne Newton—"Daddy Don't You Walk So Fast"
Laura Nyro—*New York Tendaberry*
Tony Orlando—*Bless You* / "Will You Love Me Tomorrow" / "My Baby's A Stranger" / "My Mother" / "Loving Touch" / "Some Kind Of Wonderful" / "Talking About You" / "Dream Lover"
Patti LaBelle & The Bluebells—*Over The Rainbow*
Tom Paxton—*Heroes*
Johnny Pinapple—*Fresh Johnny Pinapple*
Gene Pitney—*It Hurts To Be In Love / The Pick Of Gene Pitney* / "Every Breath I Take" / *World Wide Winners*
Platters—"My Prayer" / "Great Pretender"
Arthur Prysock—"April In Paris" / "When I Fall In Love" / "I'm Glad There Is You"
Johnny Rae—"Walking In The Rain"
Della Reese—"A Far Better Thing" / "All The World Loves A Lover"
Jimmy Ricks—"Hi Lily, Hi Lo" / "Young At Heart"
Stan Rubin—*Open House* / "Tiger Town 5" / *The Ivy League Jazz Band Ball*
Ruby & The Romantics—"Our Day Will Come"
Bobby Rydell—"Forget Him" / "Wild One" / "I'll Never Dance Again" / "If It Hadn't Been For You" / "Every Little Something" / "Don't Take Me For Granted"
Freddie Scott—"Hey Girl"
Hazel Scott—"St. Louis Blues" / "After Hours" / "My Little Guy"
Neil Sedaka—"Calendar Girl" / "Breaking Up Is Hard To Do" / "Happy Birthday Sweet 16" / *Little Devil*
Shangri-las—"Remember Walking In The Sand"
The Shirells—"Will You Still Love Me Tomorrow" / "It's Love That Counts" / "What's The Matter" / "I Didn't Mean To Hurt You"
Simon & Garfunkel—"The Boxer" / "Frank Lloyd Wright"
Joanie Summers—"I Need Your Love" / "Johnny Get Angry" / "Summer Place" / "Shake Hands With A Fool" / "Since Randy Moved Away"
The Three Sons—*16 Greatest Hits / Country Music Shindig / Fun In The Sun*
Tippie & The Clovers—"Bossa Nova Baby"
Sammy Turner—"Lavender Blue"
June Valli—"Hush Little Baby" / "I'm Afraid"
Bobby Vinton—"Always In My Head" / "I Fall To Pieces" / "I Can't Help It" / "I Can't Stop Loving You" / "Please Help Me I'm Falling" / *Blue On Blue* / "Blue Velvet" / "Nobody Asking Questions" / "Roses Are Red" / "Over And Over" / "You're Losing Your Baby" / "Alone" / "Mr. Lonely"
Adam Wade—"Turn Back The Hands Of Time"
Dionne Warwick—"Walk On By" / "Do You Know The Way To San Jose" / "What The World Needs Now" / "I'll Never Fall In Love Again" / "Say A Little Prayer" / "Promises Promises" / "Anyone Who Had A Heart" / "Don't Make Me Over" / "Make It Easy On Yourself" / "You Will Never Get To Heaven"
Dinah Washington—"Mood Indigo" / "God Bless The Child" / "I'm A Fool To Want You" / "Stranger In Town" / "When Your Lover Is Gone"
Andy Williams—"Can't Get Used To Losing You" / "Hopeless" / "Tonight" / *Never On Sunday* / "Summer Place" / "Tender Is The Night" / "Help Me" / "Don't You Believe It" / "World Of The Young"
Jackie Wilson—*Shake A Hand* / "You'd Better Know"

Gary has also recorded with the following artists:
Frankie Avalon, Tony Bennett, Tommy Boyce, Kitty Callan, Jo Ann Campbell, Dihanne Carrol, Chad & Jeremy, Chubby Checker, Lou Christy, Don Cornell, The Creations, Bing Crosby, King Curtis, Danny Davis, Sammy Davis, Jr., The Jimmy Dorsey Orchestra, Bob Dylan, Shelly Fabares, Jose Feliciano, The Four Lads, The Four Seasons, Sergio Franci, The G Clefs, Screamin' Jay Hawkins, Joey Heatherton, Al Hirt, Linda Hopkins, Lena Horne, Sissy Houston, Tommy Hunt, Jan & Dean, Fran Jeffries, Johnny & The Hurricanes, Steve Lawrence, The Lease Breakers, Brenda Lee, Little Richard, Frankie Lymon, Trini Lopez, Big Maybelle, Johnny Maestro, Maguire Sisters, Miriam Makeba, Herbie Mann, Peggy March, Tony Mattola, Glenn Miller Orchestra, Mamas & Papas, Ralph Marterie Orchestra, Art Mooney Orchestra, Rose Murphy, The New Christy Minstrels, Wilson Pickett, Jan Pierce, The Rockefellers, Tommy Sands, Lonnie Satin, Bobby Scott, Pete Seeger, Del Shannon, Roberta Sherwood, Nancy Sinatra, Frank Sinatra, Jimmy Smith, Soul Machine, Sweethearts Of Rhythm, B.J. Thomas, Johnny Thunder, Cal Tjader, The Tokens, Hank Turner, Twiggy, Leslie Uggams, Jerry Vale, Village Stompers, The Wanderers, Baby Washington, Joe Williams.

Gary has worked for the following contractors and leaders:
Manny Album, Stan Applebaum, Paul Anka, Burt Bacharach, Sid Bass, Mike Berniker, Herb Bernstein, George Brackman, Julius Brandt, Al Brauon, Joe Brooks, Arnold Brown, Bert Burns, Tony Cabot, Joe Caini, Frank Carroll, Paul Case, Cashman & West, Joe Cinderella, Mike Clickio, Don Costa, Ralph Cummings, Clyde Davis, Phil Davis, Pete DeAnglio, Lucien DeJesus, Milton DeLugg, Burt Dicatoe, Don Elliot, Ray Ellis, Jack Felice, Bob Feller, Bob Finez, Ronnie Frangiopani, Mark Fredricks, Ray Free, Ed Friedman, Al Gargoni, Johnny Gart, Mickey Gentile, Bill Giant, Henry Glover, Leroy Glover, Jack Gold, Wally Gold, Goldi Goldmar, George Golner, Tommy Goodman, Ellie Greenwich, Stan Grenberg, Morty Grupp, Ray Haley, Al Hamm, Art Harris, Jim Haskell, Julie Held, Lee Holdridge, Marvin Holsman, Frank Hunter, George Hunter, Dick Jacobs, Jay & The Americans, Henry Jerome, Jerry Jerome, Quincy Jones, Ed Kaloff, Artie Kaplan, Dave Kapp, Danny Kesler, Burt Keyes, Carol King, Leroy Kirkland, Don Kirshner, Terry Knight, Steve Lawrence & Edie Gorme, Sonny Lester, Jack Lewis, Jerry Lieber & Mike Stoller, Cathy Linn, Sammy Loew, Al Lorber, Joe Malin, Marty Manning, Trade Martin, Tom Morgan, Van McCoy, Bob Mersey, O.B. Messengil, Johnny Mesner, Hal Miles, Helen Miller, Hugo Montenegro, Jimmy Mundy, Charlie Nailor, Ed Newmark, Al Nevins, Fred Norman, Laura Nyro, Klaus Oberman, Milt Okum, Lee Packrus, Felix Pappilardi, Johnny Parker, Gene Pestile, Tony Piano, Ann Phillips, Jerry Ragavoy, Walter Ram, Phil Ramone, Teddy Randazzo, Joe Ranzetti, Hale Rood, Jerome Richardson, Paul Robinson, Bill Romale, Richard Rome, Steve Rossi, Chuck Sagle, Russ Savakis, Jack Schanland, Don Sebesky, Gary Sherman, Joe Sherman, Bobby Short, Phil Spector, Billy Strange, Barbra Streisand, Craig Taylor, Jack Urban, Nick Venet, John Walsh, Jerry Wexler, Pat Williams, Teacho Wilshire, Jerry Wiltner, Hugo Winterhalter, Gretchen Wyler, Max Zeppos

Movies: The Love Of Ivy, Sleeping Giant, Viva Max, Tici Tici, Daddy You Kill Me, Money Talks, Parade, The Wrong Damn Film, Heartbreak Kid, Secret File, Target In The Sun, Cry Of The Wolf, Hotfoot, Johnny We Hardly Knew You, It's A Mad, Mad, Mad, Mad World, The Shark, The Boys In The Band, Minority By Choice, Law And Disorder, Bob & Carol, Ted & Alice.

The Chester Interview

It's been thirty years since Gary Chester's landmark work, *The New Breed*, was first issued by Modern Drummer Publications. In that time, this innovative book has become a mainstay of drumming literature, studied by drummers the world over.

At the time of its sixteenth printing, in July 2006, we were approached by Katrina Chester, Gary's daughter, with the idea of including some audio with the book. She had obtained a recording of an interview with her father from 1984, done by Danny Gottlieb, a revered drummer in his own right and a former student of Gary's. The interview is so informative and reveals so much about the late, great teacher's concepts that we at *MD* and the Chester family felt it needed to be included in a new edition of the book.

It truly is amazing to hear Gary—in his own words—offering such helpful playing and career tips. For *The New Breed*'s twentieth printing, we're excited to offer this interview as an exclusive download that's playable on all platforms and devices via Hal Leonard's innovative My Library online service. We sincerely feel that you'll be inspired by hearing from the master himself.

All the best,
The Editors
Modern Drummer magazine

Gary Chester
Drummer, Mentor, And Father

I was a lucky kid to grow up in such an eclectic and musical household. Inspiration was at every turn, with different musicians coming and going at all times. One man in particular stood out: famed singer-songwriter Jim Croce. He used to take the time to sit with me, listen to haunted-house records, and attempt to play backgammon.

One day, when I was five years old, pressing my ear up against my father's studio doors, I heard my dad crying. It's one of the only memories I have of him doing that, except for many years later when he found my diary—not good when you have a Sicilian father! Jim Croce, my father's friend and fellow musician, had died in a plane crash. I later learned that my dad was supposed to have been on that tour and on that doomed flight. As I write this, I think about how much we all would have missed had my father been on that plane.

Gary Chester was a drummer, mentor, father, and so much more. Fortunately, I've been blessed with the memories of a truly unique role model, and the drummers who had the opportunity to study with him are left with the guidance of a bona fide guru. I am so happy to be able to share this lost recording with those of you who weren't able to know my father. For those of you who did know him, thank you for sharing my father with me, and for keeping the legend that is "The New Breed" alive.

Several people were instrumental in making this recording a possibility. I want to thank Chris Adams, Danny Gottlieb, Rick Mattingly, *Modern Drummer*, Hal Leonard, Ian Hatton, Kenny Aronoff, Dave Weckl, Marco Minnemann, Ken Dashow from New York's Q104.3 FM, Mike Ricciardi (intro recording), Tommy Stewart, Mike Mangini, and all the students now and then of *The New Breed*.

Katrina Chester

Track Listing